The Truth

Earth, Health, Humanity

Izabela Hinc

BookLeaf Publishing

India | USA | UK

Made with ❤ on the BookLeaf Publishing Platform
www.bookleafpub.in
www.bookleafpub.com

Dedication

These poems are dedicated to all of humanity.

Preface

I begin this collection with *Serpentine.*

The serpent, though often feared, carries a message of life, health, and survival. That message is not just for one of us, but for all of humanity.

Each poem in this collection is a call—a call to reclaim our power, to see clearly the deceit, the destruction, and the pain, that have been sown by a small group driven by hunger for power and wealth.

We have been manipulated, controlled, and misled. Yet we are not powerless. We can rise, take back our strength, and live lives aligned with the highest good— for ourselves, for this planet, and for all of humanity.

I wish this for all of us, with love.

Acknowledgements

I thank my children for inspiring me to write these messages.

They are for their future: bright, happy, free and full of love.

Serpentine

Serpentine, serpentine,
Won't you be my valentine?
You are with me night and day,
You hiss, you dance, your body sways.

You are with me all the time,
Am I yours, or are you mine?
What's the message that you carry?
We are close, as if we're married.

We are close, we are one,
Our souls intricately intertwined.
Show me your message, give me a sign,
Why you are with me, why are you mine?

"The message, my dear", you hiss at me,
"Is one for all of humanity"
"It's a warning, of sorts, but one full of hope:
Be careful, as you're walking a very thin rope"

"Go on", I ask thee, "do please explain."
"What you're all doing, causing all the pain,
Destruction and suffering", she hissed once more,
"You need to wake up, and end this world war."

"All of you, wake up, stand up for your health,
For your planet, even your wealth."
"It's being taken away, by the powers that be,
But the real power is yours, don't you see?"

The message is clear, as bright as the day,
It's pure, full of love, despite Serpentine's way.
She's a snake, difficult to trust,
A symbol of health and life, I trust it that much.

"Thank you, my dear, I take it seriously,
What you hissed at me, almost ferociously.
But for a snake, you are caring and gentle,
And your message was meaningful."

Her presence poses no scare,
In fact I like it, accept it with care.
I take it with a curious pride,
"You are mine, my lovely bride."

You hiss and sing a song of possession,
I move with you, slowly, as if in a procession.

Our movement is fluid, we flow together,
I trust you completely now, and forever.

Oh, my lovely Serpentine,
My one true love, my valentine.
The creepy way we co-exist
Is the way I now am, I cannot resist.

And I pass your message to humanity:
END THE DECEIPT AND DESTRUCTION, STOP THE
VANITY!

Apgar

Virginia Apgar, her story begins,
A woman of science, without much grace.
She studied life with dedication and drive,
She helped babies live, letting them survive.

The Apgar score measured the breath,
The cry, the pulse that kept back death.
Infant mortality fell, and babies survived,
Through her discovery, humanity thrived.

But decades later, what do we do?
We squander the miracle, the fragile, the true.
We poison the earth, forget what is dear,
Destroying the life she fought to endear.

Virginia's work still guides us today,
In hospitals worldwide, her score holds sway.
But what becomes of the lives she saved,
When the food we eat is so depraved?

We feed our children a chemical feast,
Processed poisons disguised as a treat.
Color and fructose, plastic and dyes,
A slow kind of death in a clever disguise.

Microplastics now live in our veins,
Silent companions, permanent chains.
Virginia would faint, her heart torn apart,
To see what we've done with the lives she helped start.

Awakening

The food that feeds us
The food that is good
Is slowly killing us
Under deceitful falsehood

The meds that we take
To cure us from the food
Make us sicker not better
Under deceitful falsehood

The media that we watch
The stories that we believe
Make us completely brainwashed
With souls hidden, hard to retrieve

Awakening is near
But we must do the work
Realizing all that is clear
Under our noses, on the silver fork

Brother

The brother that is
Is not the brother that was
He's a different human
To me, as if in disguise

The brother I had
Is not the brother I have
But he's my brother
Good or bad

A brother is a brother,
And mine he'll always be,
No matter how much he's bothered
By me

The Great Transformation

Transformation is here—there's no going back,
We are all part of it, every soul on track.

Old processes fading, new cycles beginning,
No more pretending—we are all spinning.

Spinning out of control, leaving it behind,
Control held us back, trapping every mind.

All that burden is finally, blessedly ending,
Releasing us from the past we've been defending.

We are done with judging, blaming, and pretending,
Old cycles are breaking, the bullshit is ending.

We step onto our true and parallel track,
At last we are free—no more looking back.

No more polarizing, no party lines to defend,
Old divisions dissolve, conflicts find their end.

As we awaken and soften, our hearts neutralize,
We gently move beyond the urge to polarize.

New energies arrive, embracing us with joy,
A guiding current lifts us, nothing can destroy.

The turmoil fades, its remnants almost gone,
We rise beyond it all—and move on to Love.

Fret not, my fellow humans—this is the place to be,
Together we will weather it, together we'll be free.

We will all survive it, renewed by what we see,
And when the storm has settled—we'll simply BE.

Loneliness

Oh, loneliness, my closest friend
Here I am, with you, to the end,
To the end of being lonely
Which I trust is where I'll eventually be.

I know this will end, I trust its almost over,
I will find my people and I will discover
A beautiful world full of amazing beings
Ones aligned to my soul, mirroring my feelings.

Tree Sap

Gorgeous hues of gold
Gooiness galore
Transparency you hold
Tree sap I adore

Soft when you are warm
Sticky as can be
Hard when cold or old
The secret of longevity

As I am stuck right now
Empty and alone
I feel you are my captor
You are natural

So hold me if you must
In patience I remain
For even trees know stillness
Bring sweetness from the pain

The Book of Life

The book of life opens and out come the words
Natasha begins to sing them, with her high vocal chords
She hits every word with the perfect tone
Bringing out the beauty she feels through her bones

The trees and rivers dance to her song
Confirming everyone and everything belongs
To each other and everything all around
Now and forever, we are together bound

The book of life has infinite chapters
Inscribed with every soul that it captures
Spanning all life forms, every living being
Connecting them to each other, from the beginning

Even though there wasn't one and there'll be no end
As difficult as that concept is to comprehend
For time's not linear — it circles and loops
And we, as humans, keep leaping through hoops

As we jump, we learn, we come to understand
That the book of life archives all lifespans
It keeps every story, every joy, every strife
The eternal unfolding of all that is alive

Scam

Scamming, phishing, profit-wishing,
Eyes on gain, intentions missing.
Taking advantage of vulnerability
Caring only about profitability.

Where is the heart, the true intention?
The love for art, full of inspiration?
Belief in hard work and dedication,
Not just cold facts and information.

Deceitfulness all around me.
Trust no one, my inner voice whispers to me,
Into my ear, every morning.
But I don't give up, I chose to keep going.

I keep the hope for truth alive,
That out of nowhere, someone will arrive,
Someone who can truly see
The art beyond the currency.

Patience

I wait and wait, and wait some more.
Not rushing, not running, I have time galore.
I've waited this long, I will wait longer
As silence makes the spirit stronger.

My work is seen, though not yet known,
Its time will come, its truth will be shown.
I know what's in store, it's around the corner,
I see that corner, and walk slowly towards it

Once I get to it, I will stop for a moment,
Take a deep breath and appreciate it,
Before I step forward and round that bend,
I'll feel the grandeur that begins there — not ends.

So What

Yes, they exist — yes, they are here,
But does it matter? Why the fear?
They've been around since time began,
And they'll remain — that's just the plan.

So why the hype, the grand excitement?
Now that *3I Atlas* stirs alignment,
People buzz with deep emotion,
As if it shakes their soul's devotion.

But why should it? They're simply beings —
Like us, just wiser in what they're seeing.
More advanced, and keen to guide,
Not to harm — so put fear aside.

Alignment

It seems fine, it seems grand
But something is off, I don't understand
What it is but it's not exactly right
I am feeling off, my inside full of fright

My true self knows its path, is perfectly aligned
But my rational human sees another route
It needs the other route to sustain the family
But my inside scream for my true identity

It says "no" to the standard, the familiar
It wants to venture out and touch the unknown
It wants to explore and take risks
The cost is high, it wants to resist

Which path will I chose, I know the answer well
It's scary, its risky, but time will tell
For though its uncertain it also frees
The only way true to me

What Is

All that is what is.
All that was is what is.
All that will be is what is.
As all of it is now, combined. Intertwined.

All that will be will be.
All that we have yet to see.
All that we have yet to be.
Is all that we already are now, combined.

Intertwined

Comfort Within

Find comfort in your discomfort
Be patient with your impatience
Allow it all to just be
And let yourself be free

Find love in your hate
Be peaceful in your angst
Allow it all to remain
Within you, without disdain

Find truth in all the lies
Be grateful for what's tough
Allow it all to be still
And practice strong will

Normal

Substitution seems natural
Although not so obvious

What is normal for someone
May not be at all common

What's common for many
may never feel normal for any one

Common is for the collective
Normal is more personal

And the space between them
Is where truth lives

Home within

What happens within
manifests outside.
It's difficult to contain,
to keep from spilling out.

You are not homeless.
No one is.
Mother Gaia is your home,
as is the Cosmos.

Every tree, rock, and star
is part of you, calls you near,
to unite with all that surrounds
Without any fear.

Each grain of sand, each drop of ocean,
calls you home — if you choose to accept it,
to carry it in your soul, your id, your ego.
Let it. Take it all in, and let it all go.

17. Food Suicide

Its delicious, its addictive
It wants us to eat it
No matter how vindictive
The food is, we retrieve it

It slowly and quietly
Works its way through our system
Like a silent killer
Making us unable to resist it

We know how it works
We are aware
But we're unable to resist it
All we do is stare

We stare at the labels,
We understand the contents
They are slow killers of our bodies
Slow killers of our systems

We can't resist, we'd rather die
Slow death by food suicide

Health

Is it the disease that kills you,
or the medication?
Is it the root cause,
or the so-called solution?
Is it the illness itself,
or the treatment at hand?
Whichever you believe
will silence the band.
You hold health within you,
the power to heal.
You only need to know it
and dare to feel.

HEALTH

Water

So simple. So pure.
The element of life, for sure.
So simple. So plain.
Without it — we cannot remain.

So simple. So clear.
The element of emotion — a tear.
So simple. So translucent,
so gentle, so innocent.

So simple. So basic.
It can't be made or faked.
It gives — and it takes.
It moves with intelligence awake.

One day we will know.
One day it will flow
through us — and show
all that it knows. **It KNOWS**

Pendulum Swings

The pendulum swings
It circles and rotates
As if it had wings
With me, it resonates

The pendulum feels
The energy around it
Expressing it through dance
Hypnotizing me with it

The pendulum spins
On its axis, all around
Entertaining my heart and mind
Without a sound

My guiding tool
for the moment at hand
Shows me the path
Where my journey may land

The End

The end is near
of the world as we know.
But do not worry,
it's only to show

That the old must fall
for the new to arise,
So truth can expand
before our human eyes.

From ashes to essence,
the new Earth will grow.
And we will grow with it
in happiness and flow.